STRICTLY FROM HUNGER

STRICTLY FROM HUNGER

Poems by
Jennifer Litt

Accents Publishing • Lexington, Kentucky • 2022

Copyright © 2022 by Jennifer Litt
All rights reserved

Printed in the United States of America

Accents Publishing
Editor: Katerina Stoykova
Cover Painting: *Fire Season* by Richard C. Harrington

Library of Congress Control Number: 2022940883
ISBN: 978-1-936628-94-0
First Edition

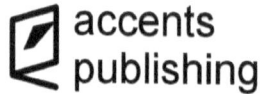

Accents Publishing is an independent press for brilliant voices. For a catalog of current and upcoming titles, please visit us on the Web at

www.accents-publishing.com

CONTENTS

I.

OXO / 3
The Great Fire of February, 1928 / 4
Rule #9: Never Forget to Change the Battery … / 5
Handiwork / 6
Boundaries Make Escape Impossible / 7
The Restaurant Formerly Known as Chanticleer / 8
Tiverton Yacht Club, 1972 / 9
Hum / 10
Vintage Plastic Photo Slide Viewer Keychain (1) / 11
Tuned Out / 12
The Woman with Medicine in Her Voice / 13
Full Moon Ocean in B Flat Minor at Dusk / 14
No Added Sugar / 15
The Demise of the Skilled American Workforce / 16
Silken Nets / 17
Altered Prayer / 18

II.

Marriage Horoscope (October 26, 1991, 4:20 pm) / 21
Engagement with Nature / 22
Climate Change / 23
We Cut Out Cardboard Footprints & Laid Them on the Floor … / 24
Vintage Plastic Photo Slide Viewer Keychain (2) / 25
Rule # 37: Always Cook the Rabbit Your Husband Shoots … / 26
To Salvage the Leeks in Late October / 27
Ode to Venison / 28
Dear Xing / 29
Divorce Horoscope (June 10, 2014, 11:04 am) / 30
Vintage Plastic Photo Slide Viewer Keychain (3) / 31
A Clown with a Context / 32

III.

River Bend, Year's End / 35
The Parallel Universes of February 8, 2007 / 36

The Moon Is a Friend for the Lonesome / 37
Buddhist Yard Sale Offers a Bit of Nirvana for Bargain Hunters / 38
We've Got Our Wires Crossed / 39
Flirting with Danger at the Art Show / 40
For Moonshine on the Water / 41
Crushing / 42
The Opal Ring Declares Her Love for the Man in the Moon / 43
Astral Projections / 44
Dropping Anchor in Neverland / 45
Ultrasound / 46
At the New Bedford Whaling Museum / 47
The Rounded Tips of Your Fingernails / 48
One by One They Drop Away / 49
Rule #86: Never Smoke & Drink When You're Alone in Bed / 50
Women of a Certain Age / 51
Miss Fall River, Massachusetts, 1921 / 52
A Bermuda Triangle / 53
Rule #92: Never Forget Your Father's Element Was Fire / 54
Mother Superior Gets Porked Again / 55
March / 56
Sea Hunt / 57
Plenty of Fish / 58
Arrangements / 59

Notes / 61

Acknowledgments / 63

About the Author / 65

for my son Max, unexpected inheritance

I.

OXO

I open each can of worms to bait
my past, wriggle truth from its barbed
hooks. Even when ragged tin shreds
my fingers. Even when guts smear
my hands. I mastered the self-fillet: served
up as whole with head intact to those
who would devour me. Notice my dead
eye, my dress of greens draped to hide incisions.

My mother refused to see a therapist, said
to pick at old sores was far more dangerous
than cigarettes & repression. Once you remove
the lid, you can't return the contents to the can.
I've lived long enough to know that's partly true.

Lovers, like fish, start to smell
after three days, but I lived with
stench for months until I found
a citrus spray to clear the air. I've dangled
my love in these waters for years, but maybe
I'm angling in the wrong direction. That
or replace my lure, find a new location.

I purchased a can opener that leaves
a smooth-edged lid, requires tiny pliers
to lift it, dismantle any bombs. Now
I can nibble at my past, replace the lid,
& preserve it for another time.

THE GREAT FIRE OF FEBRUARY, 1928

Point of origin: the salamander. Its spark,
swept by a cold wind from Mount Hope Bay
up Pocasset Street, feeds the oil-soaked floor
of the windowless mill, leaps from hotel to theater
to synagogue to Granite Block, & devours Fall River's
heart in the eight hours crews take to smother it.

Eye of newt added to the witches' cauldron first,
fiery spice of mustard seed to lace the curse.
For a charm of powerful trouble.
Like a hell-broth boil & bubble.

Dad, you inhale the amphibious fumes. Your mother
holds your hand, feels your spark & holds it tighter.
You're only six, but she sees the flames in your eyes,
knows you'll slay fires with your father's kind. Does
she sense you're a survivor? Together, you witness
the city burn. She carries your brother in utero, harbors
no inkling of her death during childbirth come October,
how you'll hold your brother's hand to cross the street.

RULE #9: NEVER FORGET TO CHANGE THE BATTERY IN YOUR SMOKE DETECTOR

because you hate its hit-a-nerve clamor when you roast
chicken thighs at 375 degrees & you're forced to teeter
on a chair with metal tongs to thrash it from its misery

because your heart-wires short every year from wild fires
set by one of the ladder company crew, uncontrolled burns
scorching the landscape & smoldering you in the ruins

because the yellow truck replaces the red truck unseats
the black horse at the station house & the arsonist reveals
his true colors every time he blows smoke up your ass

because it's your fault you don't get out, don't learn
the difference between a real blaze & a false alarm.

HANDIWORK

This machine may be dangerous to dreamers—the sign
management should have tacked above my shift
position before the finger guard snapped
my right thumb while I was thinking about
Carl the lobsterman who daubed his canvases
with Monet blues & brushed my body
with translucence, water lilies blossoming
on a Giverny pond. It dangled from my hand,
a newborn covered in blood before the cord
is cut, until the boss wrapped it in cloth
& drove me to emergency. My sister said
I planned it, so I wouldn't have to work.
The next week I skinny-dipped in the surf,
right arm thrust above the waves toward
the gauzy light in defiance of factory life.

BOUNDARIES MAKE ESCAPE IMPOSSIBLE

We're not finished with God when we leave
Dominican Academy, but our parents are
finished with the nuns' French-Canadian accents,
as if the English we speak on the Rhode Island-
Massachusetts border is more pleasing to the ear.
At Fort Barton, the public school, the third-grade
teacher assigns my sister's class the following task:
Draw what you think happens after you die.

When astronauts face the final frontier, they suffocate
on hot metal, welding & charred steak fumes to a score
of electromagnetic waves in a vacuum of plasma, particles,
dust & gas, a point of no return.

My sister hands in a sheet of black construction paper.

THE RESTAURANT FORMERLY KNOWN AS CHANTICLEER

I waited tables at the Moulin Rouge,
until I poured water on a woman's lap,
instead of in her glass. My head was
in Paris with artists & aristocrats wearing
sequined red gowns & purple plumed hats,
not this space of laminate tables, fake flowers
& vinyl chairs, one block from my house.

French words evoke the lush & languid,
say languishing on a chaise longue. I fancied
myself Marie Antoinette, head still intact,
with much to learn about serving, if not the
masses, then certainly food. Coquille St. Jacques
sounds haute cuisine, tastes divine, but it's a study
in visual banality; white scallops served in a creamy
sauce upon a pearly shell. I wore a crisp white blouse
and apron over a pair of ecru slacks.

I imagined a picnic on the grounds of the Tour Eiffel,
the water I spilled on my customer splashing
from the rising banks of the river Seine.

TIVERTON YACHT CLUB, 1972

Shrink from the commodore's horn blasting through the air · taste salt on my skin & watch the fog roll in · play shuffleboard on the broken concrete court · eat salted french fries & fruit pops on the club porch · run down the long splintery dock · swim through Sakonnet River debris · paddle to the rickety raft, climb up the ladder & stream down the curved aqua slide · step on the shell of a dead horseshoe crab · scream when a jellyfish brushes my leg · bury my toes in the hot beach sand · smooth aloe on my sunburned skin · serve as the crew in a candy boat race · take sailing lessons when I don't even have a boat · gaze across the river to the Portsmouth shore · enter a ping pong match on a rainy morn · pull on a sweatshirt as a thunderstorm approaches · flirt with Buzzy & Fish · avoid Biddles & Tag · wear my desire in a flowered maxi dress · slow dance to "Down by the River" in the dark ·

HUM

Our refrigerator hums, a steady presence,
like Mom & Dad & supper every night.
Dad called me a chowhound, & he was right.
I hummed through every meal—pork chops,
spaghetti with meatballs, homemade fries;
even my first taste of applesauce.

Having no ear for food, my younger sister
sounded the lone discordant notes—*no pot roast
touching my mashed potatoes! No gravy on the goddamn
mashed potatoes!*—& was silenced by a bar of soap.

My hum converted to a mantra for whole grains,
broccoli, tomatoes, blueberries, beans & greens.
I grow windowsill herbs now: tarragon, thyme,
rosemary, dill, oregano, Italian parsley, chives;
& the only one my sister likes—cilantro.

VINTAGE PLASTIC PHOTO SLIDE VIEWER KEYCHAIN (1)

Delmar Colorscope, 1963 · Turquoise as Miami Beach ocean · Smooth as Sinatra at the Fontainebleau · Look through the peep hole at the view · A picture of Mom & Dad has relieved the original pin-up nude · They're toasting his insurance sales with champagne over surf & turf in the Pink Flamingo Room · Later, rekindling their romance on this second honeymoon · Whatever keys opened their hearts to each other, or not, is really of no matter · Print your own photo on a transparent slide, open the top of the viewer, & replace the one inside ·

TUNED OUT

The man strumming a guitar & humming at an open-air bistro
reminds me of my first love, the troubadour who fretted chords
with fingers stained by outboard motor oil, gave me mandala

earrings & my first taste of baba ganoush, once strolled through
my den singing Fairport Convention & drowned out Masterpiece
Theater, my parents' favorite program. I didn't care because we

harmonized, & *he's the warmest chord I ever heard*. I believed he was
the one until I left for college & slept with other men, lost those
earrings in a lover's bed, & bereft of guilt disturbed the cosmic

order of our social circle, the band. The coda for this romance—
dissonant. I wonder if he still grows marijuana & sprouts, says *far out,
man*, & answers, *the moon, the clouds, the stars, the sky* when asked,
what's up?

THE WOMAN WITH MEDICINE IN HER VOICE

for Erica Hastings

works behind the counter at the chemist.
She hands me my prescription refills—
sertraline, levothyroxine & estrotrace—
designed to manage aging & depression.
Is there anything else I can get you today?
A tincture of modulation, I think,
a balm of dulcet tones.

Romeo exploits an apothecary's poverty
to secure his cordial, potassium cyanide,
poison he calls medicine, the only antidote
he can conjure once he hears of Juliet's death,
He never learns the truth but acts. *Wisely
&slow; they stumble that run fast.*

The origin of love resides in brain chemistry,
but provides no guarantee for better living—
dopamine, norepinephrine & serotonin—
What else is love? It's a wise form of madness.
It's a sweet lozenge that you choke on.

I let mine dissolve on my tongue, but it left a bitter
aftertaste like the time I mistook the dog's heart
worm pill for my own. *Under love's heavy burden,*
Romeo chooses suicide. The woman with medicine
in her voice has lifted mine. She hands me
some coins from a fifty. *I'm all set.*

FULL MOON OCEAN IN B FLAT MINOR AT DUSK

The surf crests in all directions, a jazz drummer rolling
the hi-hat on two & four, a beat that rides
the foam hiss of cymbal, feathers a set
on the bass drum with a quarter note
pulse, comps the snare to close out.
A foghorn sounds its warning.

NO ADDED SUGAR

Nestor's Candy Store is Ibbotson's Insurance now.

The grass-beaten path around Lent's Pond, no longer
a leafy corridor to amble in heat or hear echoes of winter
skating screams when we whipped across the ice,
arms linked in a gum wrapper chain.

A faint impression of two bodies remains in the worn grass
behind my house, the scent of cesspool, too, where
Billy Backe & I rolled around & kissed in third grade,
our fireballs, sweet tarts & bicycles littering the yard.

What stinks is the scene of the real crime: Mr. Sherman's
living room, where my desire for a blue popsicle came
with an unexpected cost. Did he fantasize a lap dance as
he sat me on his knees & fingered my breasts beneath my shirt?

I maneuvered stone walls & traipsed through switchgrass
to sidestep future treats, never told a soul, not my parents
or my sister. When I shared my secret with a lover years later,
he said, *Everyone has to learn about sex some way.* I froze in his arms.

THE DEMISE OF THE SKILLED AMERICAN WORKFORCE

We sat in shop class at long steel tables circa 1969,
ours forming a right angle to the boys', the walls

an industrial green mounted with a bell, exit sign,
clock, first aid kit, lunch menu, & a dozen Stanley #5s.

Safety zones marked with striped tape failed to protect
us from the hormones of our time. Why not feature

go-go dancers in the tool locker cages? The boys covered
the school evacuation poster on the bulletin board

with their pick for the Playboy Bunny of the Month award.
We knew little of Gloria Steinem, the warning flags raised

by her undercover stint in a Chicago club, but contradiction
flourished in our marrow. We demanded praise for our smarts

& commanded it for our looks. Punching holes in metal to make
hooks—beside the point. A Simplicity pattern was my downfall

in home economics, my imprecision with straight pins & shears
surpassed only by my fumbling attempts to thread a bobbin.

My A-line skirt turned out snug at the hips, loose at the waist,
a V-sign miscreant lost between military victory & hippie peace.

Cooking Spanish Rice Pronto was even worse. Inside the kitchen
cabinets were crumbs & dead flies we brushed onto the counter

with our ingredients, inspiring us to dub the dish Spanish Flies.
The boys chased us around, tried to insert forkfuls in our mouths.

Once I wore lavender hot pants & twirled for my algebra teacher,
but I also solved linear equations & earned straight A's in his class.

Later, I plotted points & graphed coordinates on the X & Y axes,
found no straight lines through puberty, no way to connect the dots.

SILKEN NETS

In the gym by the bleachers,
I would flutter through the season,
limbs waving & whirling in lines & circles
for the near-men targeting their aerial nets.

I applauded their dewy muscles, sprawling angles,
splashy uniforms like tropical flowers on display.
I could have drowned in the embalming nectar
of those athletes posed as flowers,
been pinned, splayed, displayed in their prized collection
like a trophy in a locked glass case.

But like a viceroy, I eluded their tangled nets.
I spread my viceroy wings, mistaken for a monarch's,
& hovered above the court,
leaving only the dust of my scales
as delicate as hothouse blossoms.

ALTERED PRAYER

As once my mother smacked me in the face
for smirking in our church pew during Communion,
humility will enter me through the disfiguring
bunion of my left foot, along my perfect arch
& taper to the blood-red nails of my toes.
& if I ever forgive her, she'll never know.

II.

MARRIAGE HOROSCOPE (OCTOBER 26, 1991, 4:20 PM)

You were born with the sun in Scorpio & Pisces rising, but don't be
    fooled
by the appearance of sensitive, dreamlike intensity. The moon controls
    the
shots from its launch pad in the unconscious—instincts, imagination,
    intuition
—& this one's traveling through Gemini, mutable air, sign of Mercury
    & the
twins, oh quick, bright & chatty one, so easily bored & such an agile
    mind.
A risky day for big decisions. High winds & floods predicted. Perhaps a
    hurricane.

ENGAGEMENT WITH NATURE

I moved in before the storm, unprepared
for its treachery—gnarled fingers laden

by diamonds of ice cracked & fell, pulled
down power lines. We did our best

to generate heat, ran hot & cold, water
struggling through pipes. Slow to thaw

when spring arrived, I was a grapevine
with fruit formed the previous year,

buds clustered, concealed, but alive.
It wasn't a good year for wine.

CLIMATE CHANGE

I met you when you were four & packed
on your father's back. We foot-plowed
through the Southern Tier in early April

snow. You studied me with caution, until
you began to thaw. Your fingers combed
my hair while I read *Where the Wild Things Are*.

When reluctant spring arrived with all its
fuss & bother, I became your second mother
& blossomed to the role. There was no late
freeze to burn what's fragile inside us.

*WE CUT OUT CARDBOARD FOOTPRINTS & LAID THEM
ON THE FLOOR SO WE COULD LEARN TO DANCE THE FOX
TROT FOR MY WEDDING TO YOUR FATHER*

You wore your mother's death
on a long face, but your eyes
were bright as hyacinths.

VINTAGE PLASTIC PHOTO SLIDE VIEWER KEYCHAIN (2)

Memorial Art Gallery, 1991 · You wear a white tuxedo jacket & tailored black pants · You're Casablanca Rick as we glide to a quartet · Grandma Sandy calls you *alte kopf*, old head · Grandma Esther sees your dead mother's face instead · Your father & his friends put flower pasties on a mannequin · My parents are relieved I finally hooked a man · When I straighten your bow tie, you place your arms around my neck · *You begged your father to marry me*, I say · Your response: *Who listens to a five-year old anyway?* ·

RULE # 37: ALWAYS COOK THE RABBIT YOUR HUSBAND SHOOTS IN THE HAVAHART TRAP

He blew off your head, which blew
my mind, chopped off your legs & tail,
removed your jacket, cut out your guts,
lungs & heart; jointed your parts,
scrubbed & wrapped you in butcher scroll
& shoved you in the fridge. I turned you
into a carbonnade braised in onions & ale
to bring out your sweetness, soften your flesh.
What I brought to the table was never enough.

TO SALVAGE THE LEEKS IN LATE OCTOBER

I removed my gloves to get a good
grip on each one, pulling & pulling,
nearly fell down, my hands numbing,
while the leeks warmed to my touch.
I could grill them in newspaper to serve
with a romesco sauce or sauté them in
butter, cayenne & cream to bake into
a *gratin de poireaux*, savor their delicate taste.
My husband complained about the ones
I broke in two, but what he tried to feed
me I no longer swallowed. As if I were a
savage reaper & he, the salvager of love.

ODE TO VENISON

I'm the doe my husband wanted to be tender,
the one he dispatched with one clean shot, whose heart
he sacrificed to Artemis for the hunt. After butchering,
he sautéed medallions of my loin in butter & rosemary,
devoured my tenderness with a glass of red wine. He never
understood why I quit the creature comforts of home or
how interior weather erodes the foundation of a love.
He was so determined to pierce my heart.

DEAR XING

The congestion of local traffic
burns the air, as one old
tractor sprays wedding cake
that rimes the shoulders;
The Hunt Is Over topper
bent like a broken fender
in a ditch. Once upon
a time, happily ever after,
sweet confections, sudden
collisions of the first kiss
& the last.

DIVORCE HOROSCOPE (JUNE 10, 2014, 11:04 AM)

You were born with the sun in Gemini & Leo rising, always trying to fool
others with witty repartee punctuated by the lion's roar. The moon embodies
the cycle & rhythms of time—immortality, enlightenment, eternity—in the fixed
water sign of Scorpio, of plutonium moods, a true friend, but ruthless, suspicious
and difficult to understand. A perfect day for regeneration. Black-eyed Susan vines
flourish in window boxes. You'd better prepare yourself for winter or perish.

VINTAGE PLASTIC PHOTO SLIDE VIEWER KEYCHAIN (3)

Brooklyn Courthouse, 2016 · *Love is not love which alters when it alteration finds* · Unless to alter your wedding apparel or to remove the words *God* & *forever* from your vows · The concept of *forever*, hubris in your mind · Humus is what matters, the soil that breeds lavender, peonies & eucalyptus for the bouquet & boutonnière · Your love is a garden, a flourishing ecosystem sustained by minimal tillage & natural pest control · You sign the marriage register before you discover *In God We Trust* stenciled in black letters on the courtroom wall

A CLOWN WITH A CONTEXT

after Stephen Dunn

At our son's wedding
he wears a striped bow tie,
seersucker suit, beribboned
straw hat, & pontoon shoes.

I can tell you only this:
He opens his exploding wallet.
He flashes his applause sign.
His circus getup is his riot gear.

*… this clown began waving his hands
with those big white gloves
that clowns wear, … had something
apparently urgent to tell you*

about unbearable loss—
the flower in his lapel squirts
tears when he traces the planes
of his son's face, bones of his
dead wife, immortalized, no room
left for me in this big crowded tent.

III.

RIVER BEND, YEAR'S END

Wood storks pose, the Cooper's Hawk soars,
the blue heron preens & sand cranes
divot for grubs on the manicured greens.
It's chaos at the fountain.
It's strictly for the birds.
Early bird specials begin at dawn & end at dusk.

The invasion of the snowbirds seems to happen overnight.
In late December, they congregate in open carts
all around the course. With plaid plumes & red-streaked
beaks, the men carry metal clubs, hit lime green balls
& attempt to sink them into holes.
After the round, they drive off in search of food.
It's chaos at Café Fountain.
It's strictly for the birds.
Early bird specials run from 4:00 to 6:00 p.m.

The feathers belt birdsong 'til midnight;
the invaders sing chorus & verse of some
Florida folkie's rendition of *Auld Lang Syne*.
Worms for food, food for worms,
it doesn't really matter. Who will mourn
them when they're gone?
Death is for the birds.

THE PARALLEL UNIVERSES OF FEBRUARY 8, 2007

Before you stopped talking, Mom, you murmured, *A boat, riding in a boat.* Tequesta weather, spitting through thick air like the summer morning I bailed out the Dandy Dan, your brother's candy boat, on the Sakonnet River, sail flapping in the wind, before we heeled above the waves, nearly keeled over. *A boat.* You were a hostess at the Naval Officer's Club, greeting future senators & CEOs, where destroyers loomed as backdrop in Newport Harbor, accelerated matters of love, while you necked in a car or strolled barefoot by the shore, the officer who understood his power whispering in your ear.

Before she stopped breathing, Anna Nicole Smith gambled for the jackpot at the Hard Rock Casino, Room 607, lost her shirt to Mickey Finn, taking three tablespoons instead of one, along with her opiates & other sedatives. Her death was ruled an accident; no saving this sad life of artifice, which came as no surprise. As flashy as slot machines in the high roller room, she set off bells & whistles, but most of the time, she lost.

Before you stopped breathing, Mom, we gathered around you, a circle of hands, to witness the end of your voyage. Your body was a map of indignities, not the tiny X-marks-the-spots of well-placed nips & tucks, a star's scars. You received shoddy reconstruction post mastectomy & bore flapping belly skin after all that weight you lost, nothing like Anna's breast augmentation, lift & a tummy tuck. Your last sigh, a frown set on a sunken face; hers, Restylane lips framed by silicone cheeks.

THE MOON IS A FRIEND FOR THE LONESOME

When it slips behind a cloud, you return
to the poem about the dog & how
it retrieves the moment. You live

on a quiet street near a Zen center,
but the truth is you wouldn't make it
as a Buddhist, your desire to worry

the past & predict the future anathema
to monks, who create mandalas
from colored sand swept into jars,

returned to water, blest. A few stars
poke through the hazy night. You wish
you could pin one to your chest.

BUDDHIST YARD SALE OFFERS A BIT OF NIRVANA FOR BARGAIN HUNTERS

In the meditation garden at the center of American Zen,
I read the signs posted on a Japanese maple: "Let go
of your material objects" & "When there is no price tag,
please make a kind offer." The first reflects Buddha's
values—he encouraged his disciples to own eight objects
only; the second, a request for karma-based altruism.
Profits from the sale are used for temple repairs.

I rifle through a stash of vinyl, find the album, *Nevermind*.
The cover is an underwater photo of a baby boy
in the buff, his arms outstretched toward a dollar bill
floating in a pool, a grunge-meets-bottom-line compromise
from Kurt Cobain's idea to shoot a live home water birth.

I discover a fountain with a gold-plated Buddha, offer the cashier
ten dollars for the two. *Never throw out the baby with the bath water*,
she says. I swaddle my broken dreams in fleece on the couch
beside the trickling waterfall & vintage needle drop.

These yard sale donations come from temple members who can hire
sherpas to guide them to a mountain top. I've embraced a modest life
by necessity, not by spiritual design. I'll contemplate alternative gods
& lullabies, entreating me to hurry up & take my time, breathe.

WE'VE GOT OUR WIRES CROSSED

When I look out my apartment window,
I can't see the power lines for the fronds.
Lightweight statues of buddhas & angels
populate this oasis. When I squint my eyes,
the waterfall feature becomes a laughing god.
The latest hurricane passed over, but sand
bags remain in place to redirect coming floods.

The landlady dismisses the hard work of a migrant
landscape crew, before she invokes the Lord's glory
for sparing our foliaged neighborhood. The wandering
jew purples for rain in a pot behind an overturned
chaise. Scattered around the pool lie poached conch
shells, shellacked, time-worn celebrities at a sad resort.

Nepali sherpas have embraced free market practice
with a vengeance, unbridled adventurists who turn
conga lines of Mt. Everest climbers into chain gangs
near the summit. For a few thousand dollars more,
these guides lead privileged amateurs to the edge—
avalanche, altitude sickness, exhaustion, even death.

Once science took a sabbatical, it was placed on unpaid
leave. Enlightening the citizenry now sparks arguments
about the source & price of energy. I insert my debit
card into an ATM & pray hard for some green.

FLIRTING WITH DANGER AT THE ART SHOW

I yearn for a lover
with charm & luster,
to shore up my fractured
heart. You look weathered
& a bit hard, but gravitational
pull overrides my common sense.

Your sculpted silver jacks
& ball conjure the hours I perfected
my game on the playroom floor.
A pair of mermaid earrings, your
signature, caresses my lobes, whispers
tales of seabirds & pearls.
Cue the pirate to appear.

Your right hand clasping my arm
feels like an invitation, a story
to unfold, like my son's crew team
rowing at Henley-on-Thames,
why I'll spend a fortune to order
your "Silver Sculler on Agate River,"
or else be forced to walk the plank.

You say you'll take my treasure
& sail for your offshore lair.
I'll follow you there, smooth
your wayward hair, while you bury
your face in my cleavage.
It'll be our pleasure.

FOR MOONSHINE ON THE WATER

If you were bold enough to send him
photos of your breasts via smartphone,
not just quick pics, but composed orbs,
full moons with no sky to inhabit,
you'll have to maintain a façade of
take him or leave him, no casting
beyond the moon after coupling for
a gold ring & the exchange of vows.

You scold yourself for delivering your
moon pies into cyberspace, dessert far
too great an effort for that rapscallion, that
moonraker. But you moon over him anyway
as you did with your first love, staring
out the bay window in case he drove his van
past your childhood house.

CRUSHING

On midsummer nights, we drove
to Horseneck Beach to drink cheap
wine & chase the boys from Stone
Bridge, their delinquency foreplay

to us local girls. Ours were unrequited
crushes, sharp as shells & broken beer
bottles, crushes as hot as the bonfire
blaze. We loitered in my Mustang for

liquid courage & then spilled onto the sand
toward the circle of seduction. What a joke.
These stoned boys teetered beside the embers
& rebuffed our moves. They called the shots.

These boys' clubs were forever closed to us.
We felt crushed, muttered spells beneath
our breaths & a buck moon to exact
our revenge, extinguish our desires.

THE OPAL RING DECLARES HER LOVE FOR THE MAN IN THE MOON

I'm a little lax in my setting,
a bit soft on you.
Now what should I do?
Moon, you're an old soul,
& I come from an antique shop,
my golden filigree intact.
When you shine your light on me,
I'm a star, a prism, a tear, a dance.
It's all your fault I'm filled with notions
of romance, so don't reflect
on my flaws. Moon: wax.

ASTRAL PROJECTIONS

Dandelion clocks cling to the porch screen,
float across my retina after restless sleep.
Beside my futon, bent spines of paperbacks,
The Teachings of Don Juan & *Be Here Now*,

& I'm back in your pad above the garage,
silvery exposed fiberglass, a psychedelic
backdrop for Stratocaster, Martin, fuzz box pedal
décor. While the turntable spins "Ripple," I discard
my clothes beside your mattress on the floor
low lit by moon stream & stars. I cling
to nothing, so I will have nothing to defend.

DROPPING ANCHOR IN NEVERLAND

Tiger lilies sprawl in afternoon drowse, line
the path to his lair. No crocodile in sight,
but there has to be a hook somewhere. The rogue
I love has no shadow, so I never see him arrive.
He steals me to his bed & we rock to the notes
of the rushing creek, until I'm all fairy dust & tink.

He takes my hand & we maneuver the moss-
covered slope to submerge in the cove below.
He's all, *Darling, this* & *Darling, that*, as we glance
off debris into each other's arms. *A mermaid
lagoon*, I whisper in his ear. *Oh, how sweet.* A shadow
crosses his brow. *They'll sweetly drown you if you get too close.*
He turns his attention to logjams & nettles. Of course,
he means me & doesn't see mermaids are manatees.

ULTRASOUND

> Weather abroad/And weather in the heart alike come on/Regardless of prediction.
>
> —Adrienne Rich

My heart, a troubled region, vessels
collecting & removing debris; sound
wave images of turbulent blood
flow in green—Phuket shore flora
moments before a tsunami.

My blood, surging in dangerous
directions, consumes whatever
blocks its trajectory, disgorges
what it swallows. I say—to hell
with prediction in any form.

Circulation goes retrograde: arterial
microbursts, clouded venules, capillary
spouts; a meteorologist's perfect storm
dream—a nightmare for my cardiologist.
He prescribes me a beta blocker.

My clairvoyant foresees heartbreak
on the romantic front—suggests creative
journaling & rose petal tea. I write about
the sea, start *chlorophyll-drunk phytoplankton
fluorescence* & end *after-storm green*.

AT THE NEW BEDFORD WHALING MUSEUM

I found my father a wheelchair.
The footrest had dropsy;
every time we crossed a threshold
into another room his right foot,
missing its baby toe, scraped the floor.
We surveyed the giant skeletons of whales—
sperm, humpback, blue—suspended
from the atrium ceiling. Below us,
the staff set up tables and chairs
for a wedding reception.
When Dad saw the female
right whale with fetus, he whispered,
Your mother had a miscarriage
when we were first married.
Later, he lifted an exhibit phone
to listen to a whale song.
You're no Tony Bennett, he yelled
into the handset.

THE ROUNDED TIPS OF YOUR FINGERNAILS

You used to dip the teaspoon's shallow bowl
into the sugar, raise the handle to the rim & *tap,
clink, tap*, to sift the sweetness smooth.
You measured your life like vermouth

whispered over gin. Dad teased you
about your precision, hid your jigger
in a cluttered kitchen drawer. You've got
a month, maybe less—meatloaf

& mashed potatoes, two or three
tiny bites. The night nurse won't give you
a milkshake. Clear liquids only, she says.
In that case, make it a Beefeater martini.

Your hair's as soft as eider down;
your skin glows. The afternoon shadows
the rounded tips of your fingernails.
I stroke the half-moons, tap the fine bone

plates, smooth the folding skin.
Your fingernails are a high cream tea.
You raise a pinky when I cup your hand.

ONE BY ONE THEY DROP AWAY

My mother's gone, my father's heart a destroyer
torpedoed at sea. His pleural cavern floods
with fiery debris.
                      Oh, Portunus,
turn your dolphin toward this harbor, come
to this sailor's aid. Provide him safe
passage, for what I believe is this—
my father's becoming a fish.

RULE #86: NEVER SMOKE & DRINK
WHEN YOU'RE ALONE IN BED

because the brain hemorrhage strikes, the cigarette ignites
the liquor that flambés the mattress, catches the curtains, sets
off the alarm that alerts the neighbors who call the fire barn.

because the fire station relies on small town volunteers
who may be selling life insurance or used cars & answer
late to location numbers blasted by the air-powered horn.

because your husband's playing piano on the Fall River-
to-Bermuda line, your best friend Lily will curl up & wither,
& your grandchildren yearn to know you better.

because your beauty's now an old wives' tale, party girls
age out of their vices or sizzle & you're visited by ghosts
unfurling in smoke when you light up another one in bed.

WOMEN OF A CERTAIN AGE

consider their attachments on a daily
basis—living alone, taking early
retirement & self-actualization.

consider their attachments on a weekly
basis—certain habits they've acquired
—negative thinking, drinking too much
wine & exercising less than ever.

consider their attachments on a monthly
basis—the lies they've dined on for years
—the way to a man's heart, inner beauty
& superior actuarial tables.

consider their attachments on a yearly
basis—the body parts they never
used to fear—uterus & ovaries,
breasts, appendix & gall bladder.

consider their attachments,
contemplate their lack of religious faith,
obsess about mortality to the point of paralysis.

MISS FALL RIVER, MASSACHUSETTS, 1921

Baba was Irish,
but she drank Scotch.
She sipped by the hour this mighty liquor,
which rolled down her throat in waterfalls of sadness
that could make a priest squirm at the confessional door.

Baba—silky blonde hair turned to mulch, face hardened
like an untilled garden, a chin spiked with scattered weeds.
Her hands folded, not in prayer, but around a highball glass,
where she drowned her sins in a spirit of reflection.

A BERMUDA TRIANGLE

A mermaid lulled by lapping water,
she lured her unsuspecting prey,
a gray beard who managed

his broken foot with a cane, drank
too much rum & entered her
seaside lair. What did she care

that he was the hostess's date,
or that her best friend slept
in the other twin bed. Words

like *sinful* or *contrite, a fall
from grace*, never cluttered
her lexicon. She ate salted cod

with new potatoes for resurrection
brunch. How grateful she was
someone died for her sins & rose

again. That night she stole
the lamb from the buffet
& got away with it.

She never believed
one day instead of mercy
there'd be hell to pay.

RULE #92: NEVER FORGET YOUR FATHER'S ELEMENT WAS FIRE

how he earned the nickname Red
for more than his shock of hair, a hot head
in love with blazing fires, the ones he started
& the ones he fought.

how he ran for the local school board
to control the fire your sister fed
when she back talked teachers, skipped
classes or roamed the corridors.

how he drove you from Florida
to the Finger Lakes, where love insisted
you move. *If you like red barns*, he said,
it's a great place to live—

because every red barn since announces itself
like a flaming leaf in fall.

MOTHER SUPERIOR GETS PORKED AGAIN

is what my father said about my convent-raised
mother following each episode of her getting screwed
when we ate restaurant food. At the Pier,
she gagged on fatty prime rib. The crab chowder
broth was much too rich. *This baked potato is stone cold*,
she said, stabbing at it with a fork.

Her martini at Sakonnet Point, she said,
reminded her of motor oil and gasoline.
The Block Island swordfish was thick and tough,
the fritters were skimpy on the clams.
Jesus Christ, she said, so the entire place could hear, *how does this
goddamn dump ever manage to survive year after year?*

We ate Thanksgiving dinner at Sunderland's. I held my breath
& hoped like hell my mother wouldn't embarrass us.
The sweet rolls were too gooey, the Harvard beets weren't
Ivy League, and the turkey—well, it was *strictly from hunger*.
I told her I'd never heard that term.

It's swing talk to describe something of poor quality, she said.
Heard a trumpeter use it once to describe a lousy singer in a band.

My father placed his hand on hers.
It also means tolerable in a desperate circumstance, he said.
The trumpeter's the one who got away. Now she's stuck with me.

At least you knew how to dance, she said.
I guess that meant she agreed. I didn't
yet understand a hunger unrelated to food.
She ate her pumpkin pie without one word.

MARCH

I'd like to revise the weather proverb to this—*March comes in like a twice-thawed iguana & out like a Key deer*; I'd like to rewrite Act 3, Scene 1 of Shakespeare's *Julius Caesar*, so Caesar eats himself to death on Little Caesar's Italian Sausage Pizza, because March is not about murder, but about suicide; I'd like to say to every Pisces embellisher of truth—*the fault is in your stars & the lies you tell yourself.* I'd like to clear the sidewalks of St. Patrick's Day drunks lying in their puke after the parade, give them the evil ides. Uber me to a sanctuary where the healer exorcises green iguanas digging burrows inside of me, wreaking havoc on my infrastructure & infecting me with lethargy. I'd like to protect my solitude, as the nearly extinct Key deer found its niche on the endangered species list.

SEA HUNT

My father's been confused a time or two
for Lloyd Bridges, the TV frogman from
Sea Hunt, that ancient series, who sets out on
rescue missions from his ship, The Argonaut.
An old salt like me mistaken for a star.

> He's turning into a starfish,
> not a fish. easy to confuse;
> fish, starfish, an echinoderm,
> better to call him a sea star
> with his red & orange shirts,
> his armor of prickly skin.

My father eats a crab cake, drinks a beer,
& jokes about his pedicure,
a personal service my sister
pampers him with every other month.

My daughter deserves a 10% discount,
he tells the salon owner, *because I only
have nine toes. The surgeon chopped one off.*
He settles back on the couch & drifts,
but he isn't asleep; he's had a stroke.

> His lungs are filling up with fluid now,
> & no one can save him from this drowning.
> Seawater's replacing his air. My father's
> a star, a sea star, returning to the deep.
> to regenerate his toe, to be whole.

PLENTY OF FISH

Male puffer fish create sand nests
on the seafloor off Japan to lure
females who lay their eggs
& vanish. It's sand they seek, not
beauty. The males linger
for a week. All their work
evanesces in the deep.

My father swept my mother
off her feet. She must have liked
his sand. Their cremains are living
green in a coral reef off Key Biscayne
where sweet siren smells lure
future generations to dwell.

Don't despair, my mother says
when I listen to the sea inside me. Adrift,
I whisper to moonfish & sea stars.

ARRANGEMENTS

Always lacy, no matter what,
the first-of-season crocus, blue
shoot breaking through snow
melting around the maple tree,
my white blouse with petal sleeves
worn with painter's pants, blue
collar denim blended with pristine.

A snapdragon later—scallops
of red, orange, violet, yellow,
multi-colored too, a skirted
swimsuit, polish, gloss & blush
& after sunset, with shades & hat
removed, curled up on a beach-
front patio beside a chiminea.

A hybrid gladiola now, larger,
an August flower forced to bloom year
round, yet memories of infatuations linger.
I've no desire to mask the stench of an Irish
wake with my brand of perfume & shrivel,
a rubber sword bowing beside a funeral bier.

NOTES

"The Great Fire of February, 1928": The italicized lines in stanza two are from William Shakespeare's *MacBeth*.

"The Woman with Medicine in Her Voice": The italicized lines in stanzas two, three & four (line 21) are from William Shakespeare's *Romeo and Juliet*.

"Tuned Out": The italicized line in stanza two is taken from Joni Mitchell's song "My Old Man" from the album *Blue* (Reprise, 1971).

"Vintage Plastic Photo Slide Viewer Keychain (3)": The italicized line is from William Shakespeare's Sonnet 116.

"A Clown with a Context": The italicized stanza is from Stephen Dunn's poem, "If a Clown" (*The New Yorker*, 2009).

"Dropping Anchor in Neverland": The italicized lines in stanza two (lines 10-12) were inspired by *Peter Pan* fanfiction (An Awfully Big Adventure, 2003).

"Mother Superior Gets Porked Again": The italicized lines in stanzas three, four, & five define the idiom, *strictly from hunger*, which became the title of my book.

ACKNOWLEDGMENTS

Many thanks to the editors of the following journals and publications in which these poems first appeared, some in earlier versions:

Blue Earth Review, "OXO"; *ellipsis… literature and art*, "Rule #86: Never Smoke & Drink When You're Alone in Bed"; *Gulf Stream*, "Plenty of Fish"; *Heron Tree*, "River Bend, Year's End"; *Jet Fuel Review*, "Miss Fall River, Massachusetts, 1921," "The Rounded Tips of Your Fingernails," "Silken Nets"; *Lake Affect*, "Climate Change"; *Naugatuck River Review*, "One by One, They Drop Away," "Mother Superior Gets Porked Again"; *Rat's Ass Review*, "For Moonshine on Water," "The Opal Ring Declares Her Love to the Man in the Moon"; *South Florida Poetry Journal*, "The Moon is a Friend for the Lonesome," "No Added Sugar," "The Woman with Medicine in Her Voice"; *Stone Canoe*, "The Restaurant Formerly Known as Chanticleer," "To Salvage the Leeks in Late October"; *SWWIM Every Day*, "At the New Bedford Whaling Museum"; and *Word Peace*, "Buddhist Yard Sale Offers a Bit of Nirvana for Bargain Hunters."

The poem "The Parallel Universes of 2007" was first published as "February 8, 2007: Anna Nicole Smith Dies of Unnatural Causes" in my chapbook, *Maximum Speed Through Zero* (Blue Lyra Press, 2016).

My deepest gratitude to the brilliant, kind Katerina Stoykova of Accents Publishing for turning my manuscript of dreams into a real book of poems.

Thank you to Marci Calabretta Cancio-Bello, Sarah Freligh, David Kirby, and Tony Leuzzi for the blurbs.

Three gifted women writers-teachers-editors provided me with the mentorship required to complete this book: Sarah Freligh, Marci Calabretta Cancio-Bello, & Martha Rhodes. Support. Critique. Perseverance. Patience. Love. Thank you for guiding me along this path.

Close readers of poetry make all the difference. My deepest thanks to the poets and poetry communities (both live and virtual) in New York and Florida that have supported my writing over the years and added value to this collection: Charlie Coté, Thom Ward, Gail Hosking, Susan R. Williamson, Maria Nazos, Writers & Books of Rochester, Sarah Freligh's Poetry Boot Camp Extraordinaire, The Downtown Writers Center of

Syracuse, New Ground Poetry Night, Bloom Reading Series, Performance Poets of the Palm Beaches, & Martha Rhodes's Poetry Workshop & Participants. I'd also like to thank Frost Place in New Hampshire where I took a wonderful workshop with Yona Harvey, one filled with poets who offered helpful suggestions.

I have many friends & family members to thank, poetry aficionados or not, for their love & support: my son Max Litt & daughter-in-law Maria Rignack, my sister Liz Tonkin, my nieces Melanie (for makeup artistry) & Meaghan (for party planning), my nephew Christopher (for caring), Deborah Leone & Al O'Neill, Jane & Peter Fenlon, Cathy & Jim Yorio, & Danielle Scheid. And of course, Tiger Lily, whose cat-ness keeps me going.

Thank you to Richard Harrington for the stunning cover art.

ABOUT THE AUTHOR

After graduating from the University of Rhode Island with a BA in English, I moved to London, England, to work as an *au pair* for the three children of two journalist parents and to absorb the culture. It was a year of surprises: a British ambassador's daughter added to the mix; earning a Diploma of Chelsea College (MA equivalent) in Modern Social and Cultural Studies, and enduring an attack by kittiwakes and guillemots while taking a boat tour with the Royal Bird Watching Society. After returning to the States and earning my secondary teaching certification, I taught high school English in Miami, Florida, and then adult literacy in Rochester, New York, where obtaining Education-through-the-Arts grants and facilitating collaborative literary/literacy projects with other community organizations became my focus.

My mother died less than a month after I turned 50. That year I ran my one and only marathon on Mount Desert Island, Maine, cheered on my son when he rowed for Cornell at Henley-on-Thames, worked as an adjunct writing instructor at several area colleges, and established a writing services business. Cobbling together a living was both freeing and frightening, but it did give me time to write—with poetry gradually edging out fiction. To be closer to my family, I relocated to Fort Lauderdale. Writing and revising *Strictly from Hunger* has taken me several years, but I've enjoyed all aspects of this undertaking. I look forward to new adventures.

www.ingramcontent.com/pod-product-compliance
Lightning Source LLC
Chambersburg PA
CBHW030200100526
44592CB00009B/376